SAFE HOUSE

by Lorna French

⫴SAMUEL FRENCH⫴

FOR AMATEUR PRODUCTION ENQUIRIES

UNITED KINGDOM AND WORLD
EXCLUDING NORTH AMERICA
licensing@concordtheatricals.co.uk
020-7054-7298

Each title is subject to availability from Concord Theatricals,
depending upon country of performance.

---

written permission of the publisher. No one shall share this title, or part of this title, to any social media or file hosting websites.

The moral right of Lorna French to be identified as author of this work has been asserted in accordance with Section 77 of the Copyright, Designs and Patents Act 1988.

USE OF COPYRIGHTED MUSIC

A licence issued by Concord Theatricals to perform this play does not include permission to use the incidental music specified in this publication. In the United Kingdom: Where the place of performance is already licensed by the PERFORMING RIGHT SOCIETY (PRS) a return of the music used must be made to them. If the place of performance is not so licensed then application should be made to PRS for Music (www.prsformusic.com). A separate and additional licence from PHONOGRAPHIC PERFORMANCE LTD (www. ppluk.com) may be needed whenever commercial recordings are used. Outside the United Kingdom: Please contact the appropriate music licensing authority in your territory for the rights to any incidental music.

USE OF COPYRIGHTED THIRD-PARTY MATERIALS

Licensees are solely responsible for obtaining formal written permission from copyright owners to use copyrighted third-party materials (e.g., artworks, logos) in the performance of this play and are strongly cautioned to do so. If no such permission is obtained by the licensee, then the licensee must use only original materials that the licensee owns and controls. Licensees are solely responsible and liable for clearances of all third-party copyrighted materials, and shall indemnify the copyright owners of the play(s) and their licensing agent, Concord Theatricals Ltd., against any costs, expenses, losses and liabilities arising from the use of such copyrighted third-party materials by licensees.

IMPORTANT BILLING AND CREDIT REQUIREMENTS

If you have obtained performance rights to this title, please refer to your licensing agreement for important billing and credit requirements.

CHARACTERS

DC TOMMY DAVIS – 27 years old. He is a policeman. Husband of Alex, step-father of Hannah.

ALEX DAVIS – 31 years old. Wife of Tommy and mother to Hannah.

STEPH DAVIS – 25 years old. She is a self-employed jewellery maker. Sister of Tommy.

HANNAH DAVIS – 15-year-old daughter of Alex and step-daughter of Tommy.

KELLY PALMER – 22-year-old male prisoner.

DCI DAVE LONGMAN – 41 years old. Tommy's superior officer. Friend to both Tommy and Alex.

SETTING

The present day.

TIME

Action takes place over one night and early morning.

AUTHOR'S NOTES

All of the action occurs in the present day. Scenes Two, Three, Five, Seven, Ten and Thirteen are all one long continuous interrogation spanning over one night and early morning. This interrogation does not occur in time simultaneously with the family story but occurs in time between Scenes One and Three. The second time period is the family story, which occurs over a number of weeks.

Mvm

*Dedicated to Clari, Uncle Rupert and Amai Inno.
Also, Mom, Marlon, Claudia and Jen, thanks for giving
me space, support and joy the summer I spent all my time
watching theatre and writing this play.*

Scene One

(Light up on **TOMMY** *and* **ALEX***'s small lounge-diner. It is a Sunday afternoon in early summer.* **DCI DAVE LONGMAN, ALEX, HANNAH, TOMMY** *and* **STEPH** *are present. All are casually dressed. There are signs in the room that a lunch eaten at the dining table has recently ended. Maybe there is some unused cutlery still on the table, along with a few side plates, unused napkins, and a few of those present have a mix of empty or partially filled glasses of juice within their reach. The assembled group are playing cards. All play individually except* **TOMMY** *and* **STEPH** *who are playing as a team.)*

HANNAH. *(She slams down a card triumphantly.)* Close. I win. *(Picking up the pack of cards and shuffling them.)* My deal.

> *(***HANNAH*** *shuffles the cards carefully but awkwardly. Most of the cards slip out of the pack in both hands and/)*

ALEX. /*(As she enters.)* Don't need you doing that, making excuses.

TOMMY. Wasn't.

> *(He gets up from* **HANNAH** *and takes* **ALEX***'s previous seat on the opposite side of the table so* **ALEX** *is forced to take the one he has vacated. Everyone, including* **HANNAH** *notices what he has done but no one says anything.)*

1

(**ALEX** *gives* **HANNAH** *a reassuring smile.*
HANNAH *begins showing her mother* **STEPH***'s
shuffling method.*)

DAVE. Anyone for Scrabble? *(He holds up the board game.)*

STEPH. You're alright Dave. What about making this interesting?

TOMMY. Like what?

STEPH. You got any money?

HANNAH. *(Eager.)* Like gambling?

STEPH. A fiver to whoever wins this hand.

ALEX. Tommy?

STEPH. Just for pennies then.

DAVE. Best not hey Steph. Anyway I've got a rule about gambling.

STEPH. What's that?

DAVE. I won't take a gamble unless I know I'm gonna win.

STEPH. Can't know that.

DAVID. Exactly. That's why I never gamble.

STEPH. Just for today break your rule, have a little fun Dave.

DAVE. Me, I like rules, keeps things organised, easy.

TOMMY. Leave it yeah Steph. *(To* **HANNAH**, *who is dishing out cards to them all.)* What are we playing, still crazy eight?

STEPH. Won't do any harm. Bit of a wager. Might even brighten you lot up. 'Slike a morgue in here (**STEPH** *stops herself too late.)*

(**ALEX** *stiffens and looks down.* **TOMMY** *glares at* **STEPH**.)

DAVE. *(To* **STEPH.***)* Prat.

STEPH. Ah, yeah. *(Beat – looks at* **TOMMY.***)* Sorry.

> *(***ALEX*** gets up and leaves the room in a hurry.)*

TOMMY. *(To* **STEPH.***)* Prat! *(He is angry. He gets up and goes after* **ALEX.***)*

DAVE. *(To* **STEPH.***)* Do your brain and mouth ever connect? Ever since I've known you you just chat random, thoughtless shit.

STEPH. What can I say?

DAVE. I think you've said enough?

STEPH. D'ya think I meant to?

> *(Pause. No one speaks, all are uncomfortable.* **HANNAH** *shuffles and keeps her eyes on the cards.* **DAVE** *clears all of the remaining lunch glasses, napkins etc into one pile at the end of the dining table. He is just busying himself.* **STEPH** *sits and watches* **HANNAH.** **STEPH** *gets up and crosses the room to go after* **ALEX** *and* **TOMMY.***)*

DAVE. *(Continuing to clear up.)* They need time Steph.

> *(Beat.* **STEPH** *does not stop.)*

Alone.

> *(***STEPH*** stops and turning throws herself into an armchair.)*

STEPH. Was just going to apologise.

> *(***STEPH*** wriggles in the armchair she is sitting in. It is uncomfortable and she reaches down underneath the seat cushion to remove what is lodged under there. She pulls out a small*

Lego construction. **DAVE** *watches* **STEPH** *as she plays with the Lego, pulling it apart but then putting it back together exactly.)*

DAVE. *(Noticing that* **HANNAH** *is now watching* **STEPH***'s actions too.)* Hey Han you want to see a magic trick?

HANNAH. Magic doesn't exist. I'm fifteen, not five.

DAVE. Watch this. *(He picks up the pack of cards* **HANNAH** *has laid down.)* I'll teach you a trick.

HANNAH. Whatever.

DAVE. No go on, watch. *(He breaks the pack of cards into four equal stacks, lining them up in front of* **HANNAH***. This piques her interest and she begins to watch what he is doing carefully.)* All you've got to do is this, I'll show you.

(Lights down.)

Scene Two

(The night of the following day. Lights up on a dimly lit police interrogation room, **DETECTIVE TOMMY DAVIS,** *27 is present. He is smartly dressed but the front pocket of his shirt has been ripped and the white shirt shows signs that a recent unsuccessful attempt has been made to wash mud from the front of it. The shirt is very obviously still wet. Opposite* **DC DAVIS** *sits a 22-year-old prisoner,* **KELLY PALMER. KELLY** *is wearing an expensive tuxedo and has an air of arrogance about him.)*

KELLY. State of you.

TOMMY. Cheeky fucker!

   (Beat.)

Why'd you run?

KELLY. *(Pointedly.)* Someone was chasing me.

TOMMY. Before that you/

KELLY. / Jogging. Like to keep fit, there a law against it?

TOMMY. In a tux?

KELLY. Why not?

TOMMY. Bit sus that wouldn't you say? Not exactly running gear.

KELLY. *(Making no effort to stifle his laughter.)* And you'd know about that. Priceless, down came piggy. Ha, dropped like a fucking brick.

TOMMY. *(Begins loudly, too loud, but makes an effort to control his voice and his anger as he continues.)* You askin' for a slap?

*(***KELLY*** does not flinch.)*

Something happened tonight Kelly, I think you know what I mean.

KELLY. Do I?

TOMMY. *(Leans over the table and is very close to **KELLY**, speaks just above a whisper.)* We've found them.

KELLY. Who?

TOMMY. You high?

(Beat.)

D'ya hear what I said?

KELLY. So?

(Beat.)

TOMMY. Twenty-one times, and that's just him.

*(***KELLY*** springs from his seat; the wall stops his forward motion. He remains with his back to **TOMMY** and places his palms flat on the wall. With one hand he begins to trace a crack in the plaster.)*

*(***TOMMY*** watches him for a moment.)*

Stop messing wi/

KELLY. /*(Turns abruptly to face **TOMMY**.)* I'm not, just *(Trails off.)*

TOMMY. Just what?

KELLY. *(Beat.)* You know how sometimes, it's like it's not real, things are happening but you can't, it all seems slow, you know, like it's gonna happen, you know that, no matter what you do it's gonna happen. Only what you're seeing, what you're doing, it won't, can't make a difference in the real world.

TOMMY. Just tell me Kelly, what happened just tell it straight.

KELLY. I'm trying. *(Pause.)* There's this place I go sometimes, just to, to get out of my head/

TOMMY. /Some junkie crack house, space to shoot up.

KELLY. Not like that.

TOMMY. This space, that where the knife is?

KELLY. A space yeah, my space. All the doors off their hinges so I can be, be/

TOMMY. /What?

KELLY. So I can be alone.

TOMMY. Where?

KELLY. *(Rubs his forehead.)* Up here. *(Beat.)* The voices stop. His voice stops.

TOMMY. *(Looks steadily at* **KELLY.***)* His voice *(Trails off. Pause.* **TOMMY** *has to collect himself and concentrate hard to stay on track.)* This place you go to, when you, I mean, did you, the knife; did you hide it there?

> *(***TOMMY** *and* **KELLY** *watch each other wearily.)*

KELLY. He's dead though right?

TOMMY. Jogging was it? Didn't think so.

KELLY. Should've gutted him like a fish.

TOMMY. How do you know he wasn't?

KELLY. Just saying.

TOMMY. How do you know?

KELLY. Don't.

TOMMY. Why are/

KELLY. /Whoever knifed him.

TOMMY. You know who.

KELLY. *(Beat.)* Must've deserved it.

TOMMY. Can't just say that.

KELLY. Why not?

TOMMY. It's just not something to say.

KELLY. Is if it's true?

> *(Beat.)*

> *(Stands up again suddenly.)* Is he dead?

TOMMY. Sit down.

KELLY. Is he though?

TOMMY. Yeah, murder, double count. Sit down.

KELLY. She *(Stops himself.)*

TOMMY. What? *(Beat.)* Was left bleeding like some wounded animal? All that blood.

KELLY. She shouldn't have been there.

TOMMY. What happened?

KELLY. I …

TOMMY. I've got all night. Just sitting here looking at you *(Looks at his watch.)* Yep, *(Leans back in his chair and puts his hands behind his back.)* all night.

> *(Silence.)*

KELLY. *(Sighs.)* It's stuffy in here can you open that door?

TOMMY. Too much is it? This too real for you?

KELLY. No.

TOMMY. Then why're you sweating?

KELLY. Why are you?

(Beat.)

TOMMY. You know why we're here.

KELLY. Yeah.

TOMMY. Did you?

KELLY. You know the answer.

TOMMY. You need to say it, *(Indicates the tape recorder on the table between them.)* for the tape, you need to say it.

KELLY. *(Beat.)* I know what you think. *(Beat.)* Well fuck you.

TOMMY. You use today Kelly? Is that why th/

KELLY. / No.

TOMMY. Come on, look at you. You're shaking, sweating. Ya need a hit don't you?

KELLY. *(Slams his hand on the table.)* No! *(Gets up from the chair.)* You don't, don't understand, I'm not, I wouldn't.

TOMMY. Tell me.

KELLY. I … *(Constantly stealing looks at the door.)* I … wasn't home. I don't know. Just let me go okay?

TOMMY. Not happening.

KELLY. Open the fucking door then, I'm melting here!

TOMMY. *(Stops the tape recorder and gets up from the table.)* Eleven thirty two p.m., suspect un-co-operative, DC Davis takes a break. I need a drink; you want something, tea? Coffee? I can keep this up all night, got nowhere to be.

(Lights down.)

Scene Three

(Same night as Scene Two. Lights up. The chorus of a song in the style of ["RUN BABY RUN"]* *by Garbage plays throughout the following.* KELLY *is in the interrogation room alone. He paces, prowling around the room like a trapped animal, wanting to escape, looking at the door but afraid to actually try it. He eventually throws a chair at the closed door towards the end of the scene. As the scene ends* KELLY *finally has the courage to try the door but it is locked. His disappointment is obvious.)*

(Lights down.)

---

* A licence to produce SAFE HOUSE does not include a performance licence for "RUN BABY RUN". The publisher and author suggest that the licensee contact PRS to ascertain the music publisher and contact such music publisher to license or acquire permission for performance of the song. If a licence or permission is unattainable for "RUN BABY RUN", the licensee may not use the song in SAFE HOUSE but should create an original composition in a similar style or use a similar song in the public domain. For further information, please see Music Use Note on page iii.

Scene Four

(The following afternoon. Lights up. **TOMMY DAVIS***, casually dressed, is in a small child's bedroom; he is folding toddler's clothing quietly and methodically. There is a bed on stage and a large cardboard box by the open bedroom door.* **ALEX** *31, dressed in black jeans and top enters.)*

ALEX. What're you, what, stop it. *(Pulls the clothes he is holding out of his hands.)*

TOMMY. She's been, *(Beat.)* six weeks Alex.

ALEX. Forty-four days.

TOMMY. It's time.

ALEX. Forty-four days, eight hours and twenty-six minutes.

(Silence.)

TOMMY. I just thought, I/

ALEX. /Can't quantify it like that though, weeks, days, hours, it's more than that, she's more than that.

TOMMY. It's upsetting. This room, it's upsetting.

ALEX. But I don't know, how much time is enough?

TOMMY. I can't. Everyday, seeing this, being in here.

ALEX. Close to her.

TOMMY. No.

ALEX. Holding her.

TOMMY. No.

ALEX. Her hair.

*(**TOMMY** remains silent.)*

Touching her little face. *(She speaks with her eyes closed.)* Yeah, doing that.

*(*TOMMY *turns away from* ALEX.*)*

Hearing her laugh and smelling Rosie's smell. In this room, having her smell, holding it almost, like holding her. And remembering and knowing, knowing that she's, in that moment, she's so alive to me I/

TOMMY. /stop.

(Pause.)

(Picks up an item of Rosie's clothes and continues folding a pile he has in front of him.) Got to sort things out.

ALEX. Put her away.

TOMMY. Just things.

ALEX. Hiding her away. *(She takes the pile of folded clothes* TOMMY *has just made and throws them in a heap onto the bed.)*

TOMMY. *(Grabbing up a fresh top and folding it as he speaks.)* Not hiding.

> *(They both go to pick up the same little dress. They both hold onto it and pull on the dress, it remains between them. Beat.)*

ALEX. Let go.

*(*TOMMY *remains silent.)*

You can't bury every little piece of her.

TOMMY. Let go. *(They pull, the dress rips.* ALEX *lets go immediately,* TOMMY *holds on but looks dazed.)*

ALEX. You've got no right!

TOMMY. I didn't mean.

ALEX. You did.

TOMMY. An accident, a/

ALEX. /What happened to Rosie, that wasn't an accident, something you did. *(Grabs the dress from him, holds it to her.)* You ruined it. Your fault. *(She sits on Rosie's bed and picks up one of her teddy bears.)*

> *(Silence.)*

You only had to go in, check on her.

TOMMY. You know I wouldn't have, couldn't have.

ALEX. I was only gone an hour.

TOMMY. *(In a tone of I have heard this a thousand times and I can't hear it again.)* Alex.

ALEX. *(Beat.)* If you'd just gone in, just...

TOMMY. I know, I know, and I'm so/

ALEX. /If I hear you say it one more time I swear to God. Sorry can't fix this.

> *(Pause.)*
>
> **(TOMMY** *gets the cardboard box that is near the bedroom door and places it at the foot of the bed.)*

TOMMY. Help me.

ALEX. *(Hugging Rosie's bear as she speaks.)* I know she's *(Beat.)* I know that, I just...

TOMMY. You won't forget her. You can't.

ALEX. Just forty-four days Tommy.

TOMMY. Help me. *(He puts his hand out for the bear.)*

ALEX. I ... *(She puts the teddy bear in the box. She picks up a sweater; it obviously holds a particular memory* *for her because it makes her smile. She folds the sweater carefully, slowly, smoothing out the wrinkles.)* I can't. *(***ALEX*** hurries out of the room. ***TOMMY*** is left looking after her.)*

(Lights down.)

Scene Five

(Same night as Scenes Two and Three. Lights up. During the following The chorus of a song in the style of ["RUN BABY RUN"]* *by Garbage plays.* KELLY *is in the interrogation room. He is sitting in a corner of the room on the floor against a wall.* KELLY *is tearing a plastic cup into pieces, he tears methodically until all the sides of the cup are torn apart. He looks at a broken clock on the wall and then begins to play with the destroyed plastic cup. Throughout the above scene* DCI LONGMAN *stands in a corner of the room; he is guarding the prisoner.)*

(Lights down.)

---

* A licence to produce SAFE HOUSE does not include a performance licence for "RUN BABY RUN". The publisher and author suggest that the licensee contact PRS to ascertain the music publisher and contact such music publisher to license or acquire permission for performance of the song. If a licence or permission is unattainable for "RUN BABY RUN", the licensee may not use the song in SAFE HOUSE but should create an original composition in a similar style or use a similar song in the public domain. For further information, please see Music Use Note on page iii.

Scene Six

> *(Lights up. Later that night, in the bedroom of* **TOMMY** *and* **ALEX**. *There is an air as if this argument has been going on for a considerable time. There is a double bed in the room, the room is extravagantly furnished. There is a wooden chest of drawers and a bedside table with an alarm clock on it.* **TOMMY** *is wearing a dishevelled police PC's uniform,* **ALEX** *wears pyjamas. While they argue* **ALEX** *continues to fold the clean washing that she is in the middle of when the scene begins.* **TOMMY** *has a bottle of vodka, half-empty, on the bedside table near to where he sits on the bed.)*

ALEX. Please Tommy, you have to tell them.

TOMMY. Ca... Can't say... Can't say what he did to her.

> *(She stops folding and looks at him.)*

ALEX. Got to.

TOMMY. Can't.

ALEX. You've got to.

TOMMY. Don't make me. *(Takes a large gulp of vodka.)*

ALEX. Just say what you saw. Just... haven't you had enough?

> *(Beat.)*

TOMMY. Hands... his hands. Touching, no not touching, holding, yeah holding on, like... like as if she'd disappear if they weren't, if they weren't/

ALEX. /What Tommy?

TOMMY. Connected, you know. If they weren't connected.

ALEX. Oh God! Talk straight, why can't you just talk straight!

TOMMY. Doing this it's... *(Pours more vodka into his glass,* **ALEX** *has a visible reaction to this.)* It's not easy.

ALEX. I know.

TOMMY. *(Watching her.)* You don't.

> *(Beat.* **TOMMY** *toasts her with his glass and drinks.)*

ALEX. You can't do this in the meeting next week, can't act like this. They'll take her away Tommy. Do you understand me?

> *(Beat.)*

TOMMY. Can hear it now. Up here *(Indicating his head.)*, like a tape on a loop, again, again, again. I'm just standing there and I hear the words, like I'm... Loud, in his voice, in his words I hear it. *(Whispering in terror.)* I can see him. He's with her, with Steph. Hearing them and not, not... don't you see?

ALEX. You were a boy.

TOMMY. Old enough.

ALEX. Nobody expects a ten year old to stop that.

TOMMY. *(He speaks more to himself than to* **ALEX**.*)* I was old enough.

> *(Beat.)*

ALEX. Steph didn't look to you for that.

TOMMY. How do you know? *(Beat, he watches her.)* Now, like this, just you and me I can see his face, can explain, well try to. But when there are more voices, the social worker, the case worker, all with their forms, their questions, then I'm not sure if I can.

ALEX. What do you mean?

TOMMY. How do I explain, tell strangers about... about how I left her, couldn't go in to Rosie, not alone because of him... and how I'm terrified of what's inside me, what I might do?

ALEX. I know you Tommy. Inside and out I know you. You would never do what he did. You couldn't.

TOMMY. Sometimes, I know he's somewhere nearby, I can sense him, smell him almost. *(He drinks again.)*

ALEX. Tommy, you can't fuck this up.

TOMMY. I know.

ALEX. You said Tommy, you'd tell them, explain about your dad when you and Steph were kids. Make them understand why you never went in.

TOMMY. And I'm trying to but/

ALEX. /They think it was our fault.

TOMMY. My fault *(Beat.)* And you think that, they don't.

     (Silence.)

ALEX. A fucking case conference Tommy. Social services, they'll take Hannah, you know they will.

TOMMY. Might be best.

ALEX. You don't mean that.

TOMMY. Just thinking.

ALEX. Well don't.

TOMMY. Visiting days.

ALEX. No stop, don't/

TOMMY. /Visiting days. Me watching her, her watching me and someone watching both of us, safe.

ALEX. No.

TOMMY. She'll be safe then.

ALEX. She's safe here, now.

TOMMY. Is she?

ALEX. Would you ever hurt Hannah, do what he did?

TOMMY. I'm scared.

ALEX. Would you?

TOMMY. No. I... But I'm scared of her.

ALEX. She's our daughter, a teenage girl, only that, nothing scary Tommy.

>   *(Beat.)*

TOMMY. Look.

ALEX. What?

TOMMY. Look at them.

ALEX. Your hands?

TOMMY. His hands.

ALEX. Yours.

TOMMY. Mine, his, they're the same.

ALEX. No, you're not him.

TOMMY. He's in me, part of him, a genetic copy in me.

ALEX. Look at me, in the meeting just keep your eyes on me. *(As **TOMMY** attempts to pour yet another drink **ALEX** takes the bottle from him and places it on the chest of drawers out of his reach. He won't look at **ALEX**.)* Enough now.

TOMMY. *(Drains the last of his vodka and then wipes his mouth with the back of his hand.)* Even afterwards, they might take her anyway.

ALEX. Stop it Tommy, if you get your act together they can't take her. There's no way.

TOMMY. Maybe.

ALEX. He's old now, out there somewhere, frail and old and weak, probably dead even.

TOMMY. Dead? A dead old man, alone someplace.

ALEX. I'm not sorry. I know I've never met him but when I think of him I think of a short man in a big filthy mac, all dirty finger nails, scraggly hair and the smell of piss.

TOMMY. I can't think of him dead.

ALEX. I can.

TOMMY. He's not your father.

ALEX. After what he's done, what he's doing to you even now, what d'you want me to say?

TOMMY. Can't imagine him dead that's all.

ALEX. Oh, I can.

(Lights down.)

Scene Seven

(Same night as Scenes Two, Three and Five. Lights up, time has passed; it is now the early hours of the morning. Both are weary with the seemingly unending interrogation. Both are seated and there are several discarded plastic coffee cups on the table near **TOMMY.**)

TOMMY. *(Drooping from tiredness but shakes himself to wake him up. Looks at his watch.)* Four o'clock.

KELLY. Am I keeping you up?

TOMMY. Just say what happened.

KELLY. You'd love that wouldn't you? For/

TOMMY. /I swear I/

KELLY. / For me to take all the blame, for that, all that, everything that happened, for it to be my fault. All me, what I did, just me, not/

TOMMY. /Confess and/

KELLY. /Not you, what you did.

TOMMY. It's over, finished.

KELLY. No, what you didn't do.

TOMMY. What're you... I don't understand.

KELLY. –

TOMMY. Look, just admit what you did, do that and we both go home.

KELLY. You. *(Beat.)* You go home.

     (Pause.)

Told you.

TOMMY. What?

KELLY. Two years ago I was in here, this room like this, with you.

TOMMY. Like a second home for you this place.

KELLY. *(Beat.)* Never said it to anyone before that, never told anyone else. No point.

TOMMY. High as kite were ya? Think I know the answer. Look you and me right, all the thieving you've done over the years that's one thing, but this ... this is something else.

KELLY. Watched you then, saw you looking at me, fucking junkie you thought, thief, liar you thought.

TOMMY. And aren't ya?

KELLY. Even then only sometimes. But not now though, never now.

TOMMY. Why not?

KELLY. Stopped all that. Had to.

TOMMY. Why?

KELLY. Mum said. Broke her heart didn't it? Me fucked up all the time, nicking and that.

TOMMY. Bollocks.

KELLY. Look. *(Pulls up his shirt sleeve to reveal his right arm, there are old track marks, no fresh ones are visible.)* Look.

TOMMY. *(Beat. Is unconvinced.)* Just like that?

KELLY. I wouldn't lie, not about that.

TOMMY. Why did you run?

KELLY. Why did you?

TOMMY. Police work you know, part of my job running down clapped out junkies like you. *(Beat.)* Murderers like you.

> *(Pause –* **TOMMY** *and* **KELLY** *watch each other; it is obvious* **KELLY** *is considering his next move.)*

KELLY. No, before that you ran. I told you what he was doing and you just, just looked away.

TOMMY. *(Brings his fist down on the table.* **KELLY** *jumps visibly.)* I'm asking the questions.

> *(Beat.)*

Which one did you start on first?

KELLY. When you say it, just, like that, it sounds so/

TOMMY. /What?

KELLY. Wasn't so simple. When you say it like that it sounds simple. Easy. *(Beat.)* It was, I don't know.

TOMMY. What? Homicidal, psychotic?

KELLY. No.

TOMMY. What would you call it then, what you did?

KELLY. I'm not mad, not a nutter!

TOMMY. Doing that. Stabbing them again and again, not stopping just/

KELLY. /Him.

TOMMY. What?

KELLY. Him first.

TOMMY. Then her?

KELLY. Not her, just him. *(Quietly.)* Had nowhere to go; coz they boarded it over.

TOMMY. Your mum, she's dead too.

KELLY. The house I used to go to, to be alone to/

TOMMY. /Not just him, her as well.

KELLY. Two years ago, I went there, last time before, before tonight. Council'd put these boards across the door, couldn't get in.

TOMMY. Your mother too.

KELLY. Tried to though, got a splinter in my thumb.

TOMMY. Kelly?

KELLY. Hurt like hell.

TOMMY. You're going down anyway, might as well tell it, the whole truth, all of it.

KELLY. *(He bites his thumb as he speaks.)* The whole truth? *(Beat.)* Truth is I got a splinter in my thumb that time, the last time before... Really fucking hurt too. Had nowhere to go after that. Started using more, had to, made the voices stop, made his voice stop. Truth is ended up in here, sitting across from you, talking to you, telling you. But you just... just... junkie liar you thought. Truth is I thought telling you, the police, it'd... he'd have to, you'd make him. But you didn't. *(Beat.)* Didn't do anything, didn't stop him. *(Beat.)* Didn't do anything.

> *(Lights down.)*

Scene Eight

(One day after Scene Four. Lights up. Mid-afternoon in **TOMMY** *and* **ALEX***'s rather small, slightly cramped lounge/ diner. The room is extremely well furnished and is immaculately clean.* **TOMMY** *and* **STEPH** *sit opposite each other with a coffee table laden with their takeaway meals in cardboard containers between them.* **STEPH** *is in her mid twenties. There are burgers and fries on the table;* **STEPH** *is almost finished her food,* **TOMMY***'s is still untouched.* **TOMMY** *has an immaculate police uniform on.* **STEPH** *has bright red hair and is casually dressed with a short-sleeved top on that leaves both of her bandaged wrists visible.)*

STEPH. *(Popping some fries into her mouth and speaking with her mouth full.)* Don't. *(Smiling.)* Don't look at me that way.

TOMMY. Sorry, I...just... I, how can you eat that? *(Screws up his face with distaste and pushes his take away food away.)*

STEPH. What? *(Takes a sip of her milkshake, which is extremely pink and gives him an exaggerated grin.)*

TOMMY. This stuff's so greasy, crappy and just...I did you see that place? It was, I don't know, it was...

STEPH. Ordinary?

TOMMY. American. *(Beat.)* His place not yours.

STEPH. D'ya know he took me there, a cheap dive like that. Told me there, didn't have the guts to do it just the two of us.

TOMMY. Bastard.

STEPH. That's Eddie for you, wanted it nice and public, thought I wouldn't make a scene.

TOMMY. You heard from him?

STEPH. Wanted a clean break-up, no complication, no mess.

TOMMY. You okay with that?

STEPH. I get it.

TOMMY. Fucking American wannabe wanker.

STEPH. *(Raises her milkshake in a mock toast.)* I'll drink to that.

> *(Beat.)*

That place, a shitty little room papered over so you don't see the cracks, suits him don't you think?

TOMMY. Steph... *(Can't go on.)*

STEPH. Come on, two weeks that's all I'm asking. Okay a month tops. *(Beat.)* At most three months and I'll be gone.

TOMMY. It's not me, Alex can't have, no... I ...uh, I mean, wouldn't, she wouldn't want... look I'm not saying/

STEPH. /She doesn't want me staying in the house? Scared I'll try again, mess up her cream rugs?

TOMMY. It's not that.

STEPH. What? Might see the cracks in her homage to the ideal fucking home show? Too late, I already see through her and all this *(Indicates the room's furnishings.)* trying too hard makes me itch.

TOMMY. *(Laughs despite his attempt to look disapproving.)* Don't, she loves all that decorating shit.

STEPH. Tell her I'll be good.

TOMMY. You won't.

STEPH. *(Speaks jovially.)* Okay, hide the knives. I don't think even I'd have much luck with a spoon, do you?

TOMMY. *(Grabs her left arm above the wrist, avoiding the bandage.)* Not funny! If I hadn't found you... *(Beat.)* Why can't you cover up those fucking things. *(Gestures to her bandages.)*

STEPH. *(Beat, wrests her arm from his grasp.)* Tommy, I know I fucked up. What do you want?

TOMMY. I'll help you find somewhere.

STEPH. *(She is taunting him.)* Would it help if I said I was ashamed, guilty?

TOMMY. Somewhere nice.

STEPH. I've already found it.

TOMMY. Alex doesn't... uh, I mean we, we can't have you here. Hannah, she's only young.

STEPH. Fifteen. That's not a child. *(Beat.)* But you know that. What was I doing when I was fifteen Tommy, what were we both doing then?

TOMMY. *(Beat.)* Don't.

    (Pause.)

STEPH. I'm not having this baby in some seedy rented room. A house full of strangers, stale air and the kind of fucking carpets that are pathetic and old and, and... I just won't do that.

TOMMY. Now whoa, Steph, baby? I thought, I said I'd go to the clinic I said I'd go with you.

STEPH. Can't do it.

TOMMY. Can't keep it.

STEPH. Why not?

TOMMY. You really asking?

STEPH. It was a mistake, I didn't mean it. I'd be good, as a mother *(Beat.)* better than her.

TOMMY. Would you?

STEPH. Can't just kill it, can't do murder, not me.

TOMMY. So what you gonna do?

STEPH. Can't do that.

TOMMY. How many weeks?

STEPH. Twenty-one on Friday.

TOMMY. Fuck. Steph? You've only got a few more weeks, can't do it after twenty-four.

STEPH. Fuck off!

TOMMY. It'll be too late after that's all.

STEPH. Doesn't matter, can you hear me? Not doing it.

TOMMY. You can't have a baby.

STEPH. You did.

TOMMY. Not the same.

STEPH. My one chance. I'd be better than they ever were you know I would.

TOMMY. Doesn't matter what I think

STEPH. Does to me.

TOMMY. And last week?

STEPH. *(Beat.)* I try, I do, but sometimes...

TOMMY. This baby'll be always, not sometimes.

STEPH. I need it.

TOMMY. No.

STEPH. *(Beat.)* To be grounded, ordinary.

TOMMY. Let it go.

STEPH. Can't.

TOMMY. I have.

(Silence.)

STEPH. You always run from her, I see you do it and I want to cry.

TOMMY. Teenagers, can't talk to them.

STEPH. D'you even try?

TOMMY. I'm scared.

STEPH. Talk to Hannah.

TOMMY. I might... what if I... I'm not like him.

STEPH. *(Beat.)* Let me stay, won't be for long I promise.

TOMMY. She won't... *(Sighs heavily.)* Ah Steph, sorry just can't do it. *(Looks at his watch.)* Should've been back at work by now. *(Getting up.)* You alright to clear this lot up before you go yeah.

STEPH. *(Beat, looks at him.)* Policeman with a record, doesn't happen does it? A drunk too, wouldn't look good.

TOMMY. *(Resuming his seat.)* I haven't/

STEPH. /Can smell it on you.

TOMMY. You wouldn't.

STEPH. Wouldn't I?

TOMMY. Not every day, just sometimes I need a bit of a...

STEPH. But you've let it go? Don't still see it, hear him screaming?

TOMMY. No one would believe you.

STEPH. Might.

TOMMY. I'm squeaky clean.

STEPH. You're not.

TOMMY. Good enough. Fucking super cop, what're you?

STEPH. I was there.

TOMMY. People move on, I moved on. Had to.

STEPH. What's it been, ten years? But then I suppose you can never really forget a thing like that.

TOMMY. I did.

STEPH. Something so big, so dark, kind of casts a shadow over everything that comes after. Like scar tissue, always there, reminding you, screaming that you fucked up. Does Alex know you fucked up Tommy?

> *(Silence.)*

TOMMY. *(Looks her in the eyes.)* Three months Steph, that's it, then you fuck off. *(He takes mouth spray out of his trouser pocket and gives his mouth a couple of squirts.)*

> *(Lights down.)*

Scene Nine

(The next day, in the early evening. Lights up. **ALEX** *and* **TOMMY***'s bedroom; there is a large pile of clothes on the floor at the foot of their bed. Only* **ALEX** *is present, she is sorting through the clothes as the scene begins. She continues to do so for a short time until* **HANNAH** *enters.* **ALEX** *is sorting the pile of clothes into two smaller piles, one contains clothes which are too old and worn out to be used and so are to be thrown away, the other pile consists of old clothes that are still in good condition and so are to be given to charity.)*

(After a few moments **HANNAH** *enters.)*

HANNAH. Where are they?!

ALEX. Don't shout!

HANNAH. *(Quieter.)* Where did you put them?

ALEX. What?

HANNAH. My jeans, the baggy ones with the pockets, my blue jumper?

ALEX. Those old things, they're falling apart.

HANNAH. They're mine.

ALEX. They've got holes in, you can't still wear them.

HANNAH. They're my favourite mum, you know that.

ALEX. Look, I thought you wouldn't... ah forget it, they're over there. *(Points vaguely so she could be pointing to either of the two smaller piles of clothes.)*

HANNAH. Which one?

ALEX. I got you some new stuff last week, why can't you wear that?

HANNAH. *(On her knees now sorting through the charity pile of clothes.)* You didn't even ask me.

ALEX. Other one. *(Indicates the other pile of clothes.)*

HANNAH. *(She switches her search to the other pile as directed.)* Just decided and that's it, gonna throw away my stuff.

ALEX. I bought you new stuff, expensive stuff.

HANNAH. *(She has found her jeans and she shakes them out to take out the creases as she speaks.)* Don't like it.

ALEX. Have you even had a look at it? It's more than eighty quid that lot cost me.

HANNAH. *(On her knees again looking for her jumper.)* Too short.

ALEX. What?

HANNAH. The skirt, it's too short.

ALEX. It's mid-length. How can mid-length be too short?

HANNAH. It's slutty.

ALEX. What about the top?

HANNAH. Shows too much. *(Beat.)* Tommy said.

ALEX. (**HANNAH** *has found her jumper now and is shaking the creases out of that, just as she did to the jeans.)* What does he know? That get up it's not feminine, makes you look like a boy.

HANNAH. Maybe I like that.

ALEX. But you're so pretty baby.

HANNAH. No I'm not.

ALEX. Tommy said did he?

HANNAH. Yeah, asked him how it looked, you know.

ALEX. I'll take them back.

HANNAH. Whatever.

ALEX. Seeing as you're taking fashion tips from Tommy.

HANNAH. Auntie Steph said so too.

ALEX. Steph was here?

HANNAH. Wasn't just coz Tommy said.

ALEX. *(Trying to sound unconcerned but failing.)* Last night was it, Steph was here?

HANNAH. *(Picking at the jumper she has just found; picking bobbles off it and not meeting her mother's gaze.)* 'Spose I could try it.

ALEX. What?

HANNAH. The skirt, wear it even, it's not so short, the top's not really so bad, I mean/

ALEX. /don't do that, play games like that.

HANNAH. I'm not.

ALEX. Was Steph here last night, yes or no?

HANNAH. She told me not to say.

ALEX. Alex rolls her eyes.

HANNAH. Just for a bit. Came for lunch I think. Was here when I got home from school, Tommy too. I don't know why it's such a big deal when she's moving in on Friday anyway.

ALEX. Your father knows why.

HANNAH. Step father.

ALEX. I'm not in the mood for an argument.

HANNAH. Whose arguing?

ALEX. Hey you don't be cheeky.

>   (**HANNAH** *crosses her arms and rolls her eyes.*)

I've got so much to do before she comes, I told him, I said, a couple of days she doesn't come round. Just two days. That spare room needs a good clean and the bed linen needs/

HANNAH. /She won't mind.

ALEX. I mind.

>   (*Beat.*)

I'll get you something else, something you want. You can come with me, choose something.

HANNAH. Can we go next Friday, I've got a day off, it's teacher training.

ALEX. Better make it this weekend love.

HANNAH. Why? Before they take me away coz of Rosie, that what you mean?

ALEX. No.

HANNAH. Auntie Steph says, the hearing next week, they could.

ALEX. Hannah they won't?

HANNAH. But why would they anyway just coz of Rosie? It's not like I'm at risk of cot death is it? I mean I'm fifteen, even I know that's a bit old.

ALEX. Don't you worry about it Han, okay?

HANNAH. But Aunty Steph said/

ALEX. /I don't care what that woman said. You're not going anywhere *(Beat.)* Tommy won't let that happen.

>   (*Lights down.*)

Scene Ten

(Same night as Scenes Two, Three, Five and Seven. Lights up. The police interrogation room. During the following The chorus of a song in the style of ["RUN BABY RUN"]* *by Garbage plays.* KELLY *sits on the floor against a wall; he is obviously struggling to stay awake.* DCI LONGMAN *stands guard over the prisoner in a corner of the room. After a short period* TOMMY *enters the room carrying two cups of coffee and signals for* DCI LONGMAN *to leave.* TOMMY *sits at the table facing* KELLY, *who is still on the floor.* TOMMY *puts both cups on the table, he has several empty paper coffee cups on his side of the table but there are none on* KELLY'S *side.* TOMMY *starts to bring one of the cups of coffee to his lips but stops midway. He looks over at* KELLY *who has been following* TOMMY's *movements ever since he entered the room. Still seated,* TOMMY *gestures with the second coffee cup to* KELLY, *indicating that it is for him.* KELLY *responds to this warily, eventually coming to sit at the table again opposite* TOMMY *and picking up the coffee cup. As* KELLY *begins to drink the lights go down on the scene.)*

---

* A licence to produce SAFE HOUSE does not include a performance licence for "RUN BABY RUN". The publisher and author suggest that the licensee contact PRS to ascertain the music publisher and contact such music publisher to license or acquire permission for performance of the song. If a licence or permission is unattainable for "RUN BABY RUN", the licensee may not use the song in SAFE HOUSE but should create an original composition in a similar style or use a similar song in the public domain. For further information, please see Music Use Note on page iii.

Scene Eleven

> *(The third day of* **STEPH** *living there. Early on Sunday morning,* **TOMMY** *is sitting in an armchair reading the newspaper;* **HANNAH** *is sitting at the dining table eating a bowl of cereal.* **ALEX** *places cups of tea in front of her daughter and on the side table next to* **TOMMY**'s *chair. The room is a rather small, slightly cramped lounge diner;* **TOMMY** *is sitting a little away from* **ALEX** *and* **HANNAH** *in the lounge area.* **ALEX** *returns to the dining table after giving* **TOMMY** *his cup of tea.)*

ALEX. She up yet?

TOMMY. Don't think so.

HANNAH. Heard her in the bathroom.

TOMMY. Must be then.

HANNAH. No, last night, heard her in there.

ALEX. We all heard her last night, all night.

HANNAH. Was light when I got to sleep.

ALEX. Middle of the night and what's she doing? Banging away like some kind of evil little elf or something.

TOMMY. Works best at night I think.

ALEX. Fucking sleep deprivation elf.

TOMMY. Alex! Jewellery making, doing that takes inspiration doesn't it?

ALEX. Jewellery making?

TOMMY. Can't always tell when inspiration's gonna come.

ALEX. Seems to me that with her it's always just after midnight, right when I'm dropping off.

TOMMY. She can't help it.

ALEX. Why can't she do it in the daytime like normal people?

HANNAH. Can't be an elf.

ALEX. What?

HANNAH. Elves aren't evil.

ALEX. Dwarf then, I dunno.

TOMMY. Well Grumpy's taken.

ALEX. Piss off; you're defending her again.

TOMMY. You're attacking her, again.

ALEX. See these, look at my eyes, this is me sleep deprived.

TOMMY. I'll talk to her.

ALEX. Ah, only for the fourth time, boy those chats of yours are really doing the trick.

HANNAH. *(Rushes over to the toaster which is on the kitchen counter.)* Mum the toast!

ALEX. Fuck sake! *(She goes to help* **HANNAH** *to deal with the now smoking toaster.)*

> *(Enter* **STEPH** *through the door to the lounge.)*

STEPH. Morning.

> *(***ALEX** *remains silent;* **HANNAH** *looks up, gauges her mother's reaction and is silent also.)*

TOMMY. How can you be so chipper?

STEPH. What?

TOMMY. It's just gone ~~10:30~~ ten thirty a.m., you couldn't have had more than what five hours sleep.

ALEX. More like four.

STEPH. Sorry was I loud?

TOMMY. No, don't worry it didn't/

ALEX. / Loud no, deafening maybe, inconsiderate definitely.

TOMMY. I was getting to it.

ALEX. *(Sounding bored.)* Really.

TOMMY. Look Steph, she doesn't mean/

ALEX. /I do.

STEPH. Let me make it up to you, can I do anything, make something, some toast maybe?

ALEX. No, don't worry, last time you went near the toaster, those pop tart things wasn't it? Sticks now, anything you put in just sticks to the bottom and burns, look *(Indicates* **HANNAH** *who is still trying to get the last of the burnt toast out of the toaster.)* Funny that.

STEPH. Just going to do myself a cup of tea, d'you want one? *(Puts the kettle on.)*

ALEX. Already got one, probably cold now though with all this standing around chatting. *(Gives* **STEPH** *an obviously fake smile.)*

STEPH. I'll make you another one then.

ALEX. No, I'll do my own when you've finished thanks.

STEPH. I can do it, I don't mind.

TOMMY. Leave it Steph.

STEPH. Uh, whatever. *(She crosses the kitchen to sit in an armchair next to* **TOMMY.**)

HANNAH. How d'you want it? *(Takes a cup from the draining board and puts a tea bag in it.)*

STEPH. Just some milk darling thanks.

(**ALEX** *picks up her plate, crosses to the sink and dumps the plate and it's contents into it. As she does this she also knocks over the cup of tea which* **HANNAH** *has just made.*)

ALEX. *(Under her breath as she walks toward the kitchen door.)* What's the point?

HANNAH. *(Jumps back to avoid getting splashed by the tea.)* Mum!

TOMMY. Alex!

ALEX. I'm going back to bed.

(**ALEX** *exits.*)

STEPH. Jesus what's her problem?

(*Silence.*)

HANNAH. She's just tired Auntie Steph.

(*Beat.*)

It's not you or anything, It's just... um...

TOMMY. She's not a morning person really, never was.

HANNAH. Hates mornings.

STEPH. Know how she feels.

HANNAH. *(Beat.)* Love you being here.

STEPH. Yeah, it's nice I/

HANNAH. /No really.

STEPH. Okay. Hannah are you/

HANNAH. /Nicer with you.

(*Pause – during which* **HANNAH** *begins to wipe her eyes, she is turned away from* **STEPH** *and* **TOMMY**. *She is trying to be quiet but it is obvious to both that she is crying.* **TOMMY** *appears to be ignoring this and goes back to reading his paper.)*

STEPH. Tommy?

(**TOMMY** *remains silent and continues reading.)*

(Pause.)

(She takes the paper out of his hands and puts it aside as she speaks.) Tommy?

(**TOMMY** ~~His eyes~~ 's eyes *look everywhere but at* **STEPH.**)

(Speaks low so **HANNAH** *doesn't hear.)* Look, she needs you, *(Beat.)* please?

TOMMY. Can't put my hands on her.

STEPH. It's not always like that, not like him.

TOMMY. Can't do that.

STEPH. Just miserable, that's all she is. Tense. All that snapping Alex does all the time; no wonder she's upset.

(Silence. **TOMMY** *desperately wants to comfort* **HANNAH** *but cannot bring himself to do it. Eventually* **STEPH** *hugs* **HANNAH** *and her words of comfort can be heard.* **TOMMY** *slowly retrieves his newspaper which lies in pieces on the living room floor and sitting back in his chair begins to read it once again.)*

(Lights down.)

Scene Twelve

(Two days later. Lights up on **TOMMY** *and* **ALEX** *in the living room of their home. Early evening. Both are standing and throughout the following* **TOMMY** *continually tries to close the physical space between them while* **ALEX** *insistently maintains it.)*

TOMMY. Can't... can't just say that.

ALEX. Got to.

TOMMY. Not now.

ALEX. It's time, for us it's time.

TOMMY. Not for me, not yet.

ALEX. Take it. *(Holds out her wedding ring.)*

TOMMY. What about Thursday, the case conference?

ALEX. If you're not there... you said yourself you can't do it, tell them about Steph and you, why you couldn't go in. *(Beat.)* I can't lose her Tommy.

TOMMY. Neither can I?

ALEX. She looks away from him and is uncomfortable meeting his gaze.

TOMMY. 'spose you're taking her?

ALEX. *(Suddenly angry, speaking under her breath.)* Well I can't leave her with you can I?

TOMMY. I'll try I will I'll/

ALEX. /You've been trying, six years you've been trying. Now Rosie's dead Tommy.

TOMMY. Nothing I could have done anyway, not really. I wouldn't have made a difference.

ALEX. *(Indicating her head.)* Up here I know, but here, *(Indicates her heart.)* It's different here.

TOMMY. I need you.

> *(Beat.)*

ALEX. I'm giving you this, for me it's not easy, but I'm giving you this.

> **(TOMMY** *knocks the ring to the ground.)*

TOMMY. Not easy? Must be for you, else why'd you... easy for you.

ALEX. Shh, she'll hear us.

TOMMY. Why not? Hannah should hear this, hear you, doing this, breaking this.

ALEX. I'm saving you, us.

TOMMY. *(Barely audible.)* You're killing me.

ALEX. I've tried I have, but it's like there's this heavy weight on your back. Even now you won't let go of it.

> **(TOMMY** *remains silent.)*

Hannah can't pay for that.

TOMMY. Alex she's fine, she's okay.

ALEX. *(Watching him with disbelief.)* You avoid her, she walks into a room you walk out. You think I don't know but I see you. Hannah's not stupid, she notices Tommy. And since Steph moved in it's like you're disintegrating, coming apart slowly with her to hold your hand, guide you into the world she's built around herself. Just the two of you, no room for me, Hannah, no one else.

TOMMY. You're jealous? Of my sister?

ALEX. No.

TOMMY. You are.

ALEX. I'm beginning to hate you a little Tommy. *(Beat.)* I can feel it inside when I see your reaction to Hannah, you're getting worse not better. I'm scared Tommy, I don't want us to become just that; just hating each other. Do you understand?

TOMMY. This is about Steph, about Thursday? Well, well, at the case conference I'll tell them I promise, I think I can *(Beat.)* maybe I can. I'll talk to Steph, ask her if/

ALEX. /She's not good for you.

TOMMY. Steph?

ALEX. With her here you're changing, have changed. The two of you whispering secrets and pushing everything, everyone out.

TOMMY. Would never push you out, run away from you.

> *(Beat.)*

Stay.

> *(Beat.)*

She's my sister for God's sake.

ALEX. Tommy, I love you. I do but/

TOMMY. /Can't say that to me now.

> *(Beat.)*

ALEX. I have to, even now like this. Love you Tommy.

> *(**ALEX** walks quickly out of the living room. **STEPH** is just coming through the door into the room as **ALEX** is leaving, they cross paths.)*

STEPH. Alex are you okay?

> *(**ALEX** does not acknowledge her and leaves the room.)*

What's her problem?

TOMMY. Ah don't.

STEPH. What?

TOMMY. Don't start bitching, not now okay?

STEPH. Trouble in paradise? *(She picks up a flower from the vase of flowers on the dining table and plays with it as she talks.)*

TOMMY. Bet you're loving this.

STEPH. *(Begins pulling petals off the chrysanthemum one by one as she speaks.)* She loves you, she loves you not. She loves you, she loves you not, she loves/

TOMMY. /(**TOMMY** *grabs the flower out of her hands and throws it to the floor.)* What's the matter with you?

> *(Silence.)*

She's really leaving Steph.

> *(Beat.)*

STEPH. You're drinking too much.

TOMMY. I know. But ever since you got here...

STEPH. Not my fault.

TOMMY. I go to work, come home and it's so... so... there's so much tension. Wherever I am I can feel it right here in the pit of my stomach. Everyone trying to break each other to pieces.

STEPH. And you, you're tearing yourself to pieces.

> *(Pause.)*

TOMMY. Never needed so much to stop it, that feeling, never needed so much before.

STEPH. Before I came?

(**TOMMY** *does not respond.*)

I remind you?

TOMMY. Nothing to forget.

STEPH. Can't you see?

TOMMY. Nothing to remember.

STEPH. I remember. Not just that, but other times, good things.

TOMMY. Never good, just past. We don't need to... to... reminiscing is for other people, people with different memories, good ones.

STEPH. Remember how he used to, late at night when we were all asleep, he'd go out there, for hours and just do his thing? I don't think I ever told you this but one time I snuck downstairs, can't remember what time it was, must've been past midnight. I sat on the stairs watching him. The light from the garage was so dim I could only just make him out. Remember how the light in there never worked properly? He'd got the little lamp from the kitchen and I could see it was hard for him to get the grooves in the right place but he went on anyway, bit by bit till they were exactly right and he could put the wheels on. (*Beat.*) I must've sat there watching him for ages. I just sat in the dark; never let him know I was there. He must've felt me, my eyes on him, but he never looked up. I was cold and stiff by the time I got up and went to bed but I never forgot that. And I remember your face when you opened your presents on Christmas morning. You loved that police car the best, he'd made it with his own hands and you never went anywhere without it for a month. Do you remember?

TOMMY. No.

STEPH. Must do.

TOMMY. I was eight years old, I didn't know him then, not properly, what he was like.

STEPH. So you do remember.

(*Silence, both watch each other.*)

TOMMY. She's leaving me Steph.

STEPH. Talk to her.

TOMMY. You don't really care, can't stand her can you?

STEPH. Love you though, don't I.

TOMMY. We've talked.

STEPH. Really talk to her; tell her everything.

TOMMY. I have.

STEPH. Liar.

TOMMY. (*Beat.*) She won't understand.

STEPH. Make her.

(*Lights down.*)

Scene Thirteen   Six

*(Same night as Scenes Two, Three, Five, Seven and Ten. **TOMMY** sits opposite **KELLY**, it is getting light outside. It is about 8a.m., that time of the early morning when it seems the rest of the world hasn't woken up yet and you are alone in the secret world where night and day meet, in the in between time.)*

TOMMY. And then what? You're doing well.

KELLY. I told him, I said. *(Keeps stealing looks at the door.)*

TOMMY. *(Follows his gaze, then gets up and opens the door, returns to his seat.)* What did you say?

      (Pause.)

KELLY. I told him to let her go. She was finally leaving him see, but he just, like always he...

TOMMY. What?

KELLY. And if I say I can see him like you promised?

TOMMY. A photo Kelly.

KELLY. Morgue photo though, him on a slab.

TOMMY. *(**TOMMY** goes to say something, but stops thinking better of it. He thinks briefly about how to say it.)* Why are you so desperate to see him and not her?

KELLY. Need to be sure.

TOMMY. Of what?

KELLY. Make sure he's really dead. You say he is but I, I need to see it, for myself, see him layed out in a morgue.

TOMMY. He was stabbed so many times, no way he survived that. Surely you realise?

KELLY. He's so strong; you don't know him like I do. He's so... nothing can kill him.

TOMMY. *(He slips a photograph from a folder of papers in front of him on the table.)* Say what happened and it's yours.

KELLY. *(Beat.* **KELLY** *looks up at* **TOMMY** *but as he speaks his gaze becomes fixed on the down turned photograph on the table.)* She grabbed a knife from the kitchen; she'd never done that before. And the look on his face, he looked like... how could he be shocked after what he'd done? All those years, as long as I can remember hitting her like that, almost every morning she was cut and bruised but grinning like nothing was wrong. *(Beat.)* Sometimes, I think the grinning and pretending, the not talking about it, just acting normal, that was even worse. *(Beat.)* How could he be shocked?

> *(Beat.)*

TOMMY. Then what happened?

KELLY. I was sitting there watching the both of them, no, not both, just him, I was watching him, his face. I couldn't believe it, he laughed. She had a knife pointed at him and he just laughed. God I hated the sound of that. Low in the back of his throat, but the kind where you know there's something terrible underneath, dangerous. Suddenly he was grabbing her, got it from her and... and...

TOMMY. It's alright, you're doing well.

KELLY. Not alright.

> *(Beat.)*

TOMMY. Kelly/

KELLY. / He was angry, really angry... you're not leaving me, you're mine, over and over... and he was hitting her, screaming at her. *(Beat.)* But she fought him, had never done that before. I'd never seen that, her fight back just... just... /

TOMMY. /Just what?

KELLY. / her begging him to stop. *(Beat.)* Can't believe it's morning already. *(He glances at the broken clock on the wall.)* Must be really, well, really early, must be/

TOMMY. */(Looks at his watch as he speaks.)* Just before six.

KELLY. You think maybe... I know I've got no right to ask but...

TOMMY. Yeah?

KELLY. Was thinking, by now they'd've moved her from... put her somewhere else. But they wouldn't know, I mean nobody would've been there to say... she doesn't like to be shut in you see, closed in, never did. I'm like her that way.

TOMMY. Claustrophobic?

KELLY. Kinda like that, yeah. S'pose it doesn't matter so much now though, now she's...

TOMMY. She'd be in the morgue, just like your dad.

KELLY. Not together, he shouldn't be anywhere near her, wouldn't be right.

TOMMY. Why not?

KELLY. *(Visibly angry.)* He's the one, he/

TOMMY. /But you/

KELLY. / No. She kept fighting him, telling him she was going. I was proud you know, that finally she'd... but he was so angry. *(Beat.)* Suddenly he stopped, let her go, but he was looking at her you know, really calm. I should've done something... I could see it in the way he was looking at her, but I never thought...

(Beat.)

And then he lashed out again only, only he still had the knife in his hand.

TOMMY. Him not you?

KELLY. I did something then, too late but I did something.

    (Beat.)

TOMMY. How did it happen?

KELLY. I tackled him, just to get him off her, but I... I couldn't believe what he was doing and then... then I ... *(Beat.)* I did the same to him.

TOMMY. Did you know how many times?

KELLY. I couldn't seem to stop for a long time. Over and over, for all the times that he... *(Beat.)* How long will I get?

TOMMY. It's bad.

KELLY. But if they know why.

TOMMY. Maybe.

KELLY. But I was stopping him, saving her.

TOMMY. She was already dead.

KELLY. I didn't know that.

TOMMY. You were saving yourself.

    (Beat.)

KELLY. Would you have done any different?

    *(Pause. **TOMMY** and **KELLY** watch each other.)*

Will that help me? That you knew and didn't/

TOMMY. / No.

KELLY. Yes it will, got to. You'll get into trouble if they find out?

> (TOMMY *remains silent.*)

Lose your job?

> (TOMMY *remains silent.*)

Suddenly I'm not just some lowlife junkie. Now that there's something I can take away from you. I confessed, now let me see him.

TOMMY. (TOMMY *doesn't move.*) I never said that.

KELLY. Not just a junkie now.

TOMMY. I never said just, that was you, you said that, I never said it.

KELLY. Give it to me.

TOMMY. Did you really think I'd let you gloat over the man you killed? Really?

> (TOMMY *holds the photo and begins to replace it in the folder but* KELLY *tries to snatch it from him.* KELLY *cannot at first but then he grips* TOMMY's *wrist with both hands and twists painfully to make him let go. After a brief struggle* TOMMY *is forced to relinquish the photograph to* KELLY. *The breathing of both is slightly elevated as* KELLY *looks at the photograph and a surprised* TOMMY *rubs his painful wrist.*)

KELLY. I'm going to tell them all about you. This is you, you're fault, I wouldn't have done it if you had listened to me, heard me.

> (*Beat.*)

TOMMY. I would have done different.

KELLY. What?

TOMMY. You asked before. I would have done different.

KELLY. You don't know that. *(As they speak the next few lines* **KELLY** *is slowly tearing the photograph into strips.)*

TOMMY. You chose that moment, an opportunity to get him out of your life, for you not her.

KELLY. No.

TOMMY. He hurt you too?

> *(***KELLY*** *remains silent.)*

Not just when he would hit her, though that hurt. It burned you up you couldn't stop him, couldn't protect her. But when he turned from her, turned from her to you, then, a perverse kind of satisfaction. For once it's not her, just occasionally she's free of him coz he's taking it out on you instead. That hurt but in a different way, too complex to explain or even understand yourself but/

KELLY. / Stop.

> *(Beat.* **KELLY** *crumples up the remaining un-ripped portion of the photograph and throws it to the floor.)*

TOMMY. All I'm saying, I would've done different.

KELLY. Maybe told a policeman?

> *(***TOMMY*** *remains silent.)*

I can't tell you why I did it, not all of it. But you... you see me, the whole of me that even I can't explain. So you know, you must, what that's like. Being that person, hating him but hating me even more.

TOMMY. There's nothing I can do for you. (**TOMMY** *gets up suddenly and turns off the tape recorder – he is visibly agitated.*)

KELLY. But you want to don't you? I can see it.

TOMMY. He's dead Kelly. You killed him.

KELLY. Help me.

TOMMY. I can't.

KELLY. Two years ago you ran, don't do that again. You can do something, I know you can.

TOMMY. Back then if I had known, been sure of what you said. And even if you could get off then what? You'll carry it with you Kelly, him with you, closer than anything, anyone.

KELLY. Nah, he's out of my head. See that's it, you know. I've seen the photo, that's real. I made that happen. And soon six feet of dirt between me and him, not even he can get to me then.

TOMMY. You really believe that?

KELLY. Was I wrong?

TOMMY. You killed a man Kelly.

KELLY. But was I wrong to?

TOMMY. (*Beat – he cannot answer the question. He gets up and leaves the room as he speaks.*) I ... I need to, to think about this. Just give me some time to think.

> (**KELLY** *picks up the folder of paper* **TOMMY** *has left behind. He quickly leafs through the case file and then begins ripping up the sheets of paper one by one.* **DCI LONGMAN** *enters and grabs the folder* **KELLY** *is destroying out of his hands and exits with it.*)
>
> (*Lights down.*)

Scene Fourteen

(Two weeks later. Lights up. **TOMMY** *and* **ALEX**'s *bedroom. The bedroom is extravagantly decorated and there is a large double bed which dominates the extremely ordered and tidy room.* **STEPH**, *obviously heavily pregnant, is on the bed hanging over the side, looking under it. She is almost over-balanced. The bedclothes are in disarray and there is a forgotten pillow on the floor. The curtains are open and the last light of the day is coming through the window, the electric lights in all the houses will be on soon but not just yet. It's that time between late afternoon and early evening when you are saying goodbye to the day but night has not yet crept up on you. The room has a wooden floor and the curtains are blowing in a gentle summer breeze. The sound of children playing can be heard from the street outside throughout the scene.)*

TOMMY. *(Enters the room. He is dressed in a police uniform, the uniform is immaculate, he stands in the doorway watching* **STEPH** *for a few moments before announcing his presence.)* Not in here.

STEPH. *(Holds up a simple silver hoop earring.)* Made these for him, me really. To look pretty, beautiful even. Not be a miserable, whining, morning sickness, bloated, swollen ankles, uncomfortable in my own skin bitch. But be the fat belly kind, yeah fat but beautiful, healthy.

TOMMY. Don't.

STEPH. Lost one though. In here, lost it last night. *(Hands earring to* **TOMMY**.*)* Was under the bed.

TOMMY. Alex might be home soon, doesn't like you in here, you know that.

STEPH. Don't mind do you?

TOMMY. Alex does.

STEPH. She left, doesn't matter what/

TOMMY. /Might be back though, could be, any minute.

STEPH. Doubt it. *(Beat.)* You, what do you think about me in here?

TOMMY. Doesn't matter.

> *(**STEPH** remains silent.)*

Sis she thinks it's weird, you and me in here, always saying things, hinting, you know, that we're too close.

STEPH. Sick she is, dirty mind, you gotta watch that one, not right in the head.

TOMMY. *(Beat.)* He's gone Steph.

STEPH. Gone, lie, no longer here, fucking lie. Passed over, passed away, passed on, passed, passed, euphemisms, fucking lies. I think behind that, after a while those words collapse in on themselves. Mouths moving, lips talking over and over, those words in yours ears again and again, but you know, I mean you must have an awareness, got to. Dead, that's true. The rest, sugar coated, avoiding, pretending, fucking lies.

TOMMY. Not your fault.

STEPH. Might be.

TOMMY. No, just happened, that's all, just... for no reason, nobody's fault.

STEPH. Happened to me though. My body, maybe... you may as well keep that. *(Indicates the earring.)*

TOMMY. It's yours.

STEPH. Don't want it now.

TOMMY. Makes you look so, so, like you said, pretty, keep them. *(Holds earring out to* **STEPH***, she won't take it.)*

STEPH. That's half of it. You're holding what I wanted. There, in your hand. Me, a happy mum to be, radiant you know. Waiting for him, then holding him, being there, good like a mum should be. Crying sometimes, yeah, but not. *(Beat – she is crying.)* No, not these tears, the good kind, happy kind, where I can't breathe. But I wouldn't be scared. He'd be looking at me, just looking, and he'd know see, that I loved him with everything I had, he'd just be looking at me and he'd know.

TOMMY. *(Crosses from the door to the bed, he sits on the bed next to her and holds her.)* I know Steph.

STEPH. *(After a few moments,* **STEPH** *pushes him away roughly.)* But you had two years.

TOMMY. Still painful, empty.

STEPH. Not the same.

TOMMY. Picking her up then, first time I could in two years. Rosie heavy in my arms, so still... but I'm rocking her. Her cheek cold against mine but still I'm rocking her, singing to her, can't stop.

STEPH. My baby, he's/

TOMMY. / Gone like mine, the same as Rosie.

STEPH. Dead, I was going to say dead. *(Beat.)* More honest. *(Beat.)* Difference is you and Alex had two years of watching and holding, of bottles and baby food and a tiny hand in yours. Baby smiles, crawling, then walking, then talking, all that you've had.

TOMMY. Made it harder when...

STEPH. Can't even say goodbye. Said he just died, don't know why. Gonna operate tomorrow, take him out.

TOMMY. Jesus Steph you mean he's/

STEPH. / Wanted to do it today but I asked them, I said, can I have one day, just today, I said, to, to, get used to it, you know. Six months he's been with me, when he's gone I'll be; I'll feel...

TOMMY. Empty?

STEPH. Yeah that.

TOMMY. Tomorrow what time?

STEPH. I'll get a taxi.

TOMMY. I want to.

STEPH. I'll be fine.

TOMMY. Won't be any trouble.

STEPH. You've got work.

TOMMY. I'll take a day off. Ring them, let them know.

STEPH. Don't have to.

TOMMY. I know.

STEPH. Nine o'clock.

TOMMY. Right *(Beat.)* right.

STEPH. But I mean, I understand if you can't, if Alex would mind. Would be nice that's all, but I understand if not. I know Alex comes first so/

TOMMY. /I've said I will. Alex won't... with you and her it's just... look, I'll take you, promise.

STEPH. Will you stay with me?

TOMMY. Course.

>   (**STEPH** *looks at him, doesn't speak.*)

I know it's no one's fault but sometimes I think maybe... *(Trails off and does not finish.)*

STEPH. What?

TOMMY. What we did then.

STEPH. You. What you did.

TOMMY. You were there.

STEPH. But you, you did, I didn't.

TOMMY. Helped me though didn't you?

STEPH. Only after, not/

TOMMY. /Accomplice, involved, helping me plan it, helping me do it.

STEPH. I was only fifteen, didn't know what I was doing did I.

TOMMY. I wasn't much older. Two years Steph, that's nothing. What did I know?

>   *(Beat.)*

Do you regret it?

STEPH. Don't you?

TOMMY. No.

STEPH. Liar.

TOMMY. Don't think about it, keep him, his face out of my head.

STEPH. Liar.

TOMMY. Didn't have a choice.

STEPH. Could've just left, like mum did, run and never looked back.

TOMMY. He'd have found us, you know he would.

STEPH. But this, ten years and he's still pressing down on me, on us.

TOMMY. No he's/

STEPH. /Why did Rosie die Tommy? Just like that no reason. My baby inside me, why couldn't I keep him alive?

TOMMY. Rosie, your baby, they're just gone, you know. Babies pass away every day, nobody's fault.

STEPH. Euphemisms Tommy, fucking lies Tommy.

(**TOMMY** *remains silent.*)

(*Snatches the earring from his hand and drops it to the wooden floor.*) Can't have that, you and me, never have that. Even now he won't let us be happy.

(*As the lights go down the sound of the children playing outside is clearly audible.*)

(*Lights down.*)

Scene Fifteen

(Late afternoon three days later. Lights up on
ALEX *alone in the living room of their home.*
She is gathering up her things in preparation
to leave the house. She is gathering up items
such as her purse and handbag. There is a
pristinely ironed nurse's uniform hanging
over one of the armchairs. **ALEX** *is looking for*
something. There is a knock at the door, she
ignores it at first but the knocking persists,
eventually she goes to answer the front door.)

(Enter **DCI DAVID LONGMAN**, *he is dressed in*
a police uniform and carries his hat in his
hands, he is obviously very nervous.)

ALEX. *(Closing the front door behind him as she speaks.)*
Oh, Dave, hi. Sorry, I'm just getting ready.

DAVE. Don't let me hold you up.

ALEX. Late for work.

DAVE. Tommy in?

ALEX. Gone down to the shops, he'll be back any minute,
wait if you like.

DAVE. No I'll...it's not a good time, I can see that, you're
in a hurry. I need to speak to Tommy really, but well...
maybe I should wait, it's not important, well, it is but...
No, I'll come back, another time, that's better.

ALEX. *(Stops what she is doing and looks at* **DAVE** *in*
surprise.) Dave, God what is it?

DAVE. Should talk to Tommy really.

ALEX. *(Straightens up to her full height.)* Dave I'm asking
you, what?

DAVE. Should speak to Tommy first. *(Beat.)* Glad to see you two are, you know, patching things up.

ALEX. Hannah couldn't settle where we were, me neither to tell the truth. Silly really, we only moved round the corner, a flat in Glenmore close.

DAVE. Yeah, I know it, nice up there.

ALEX. Hannah just couldn't settle though, she missed her things, well her home really.

DAVE. Kids do don't they.

ALEX. *(Laughing as she speaks.)* Said she'd run away if I didn't let her come home.

DAVE. Always the drama queen our Hannah.

ALEX. Don't I know it. But no, I know what she means. Had only been gone about two weeks but I was ready to come back. Missed him, something familiar, comfortable, you know?

DAVE. Today was it that you got back?

ALEX. Last night, late.

DAVE. Spoke to Tommy yesterday he never said.

ALEX. Didn't know. Came round last night to get some more of my stuff. Soon as I walked in here, saw him standing there, I knew Hannah was right.

DAVE. Hope you work it out.

ALEX. We'll see.

> *(Pause.)*

You're avoiding my question.

> *(**DAVE** remains silent.)*

This isn't a social call is it? Tommy I mean, you didn't just drop in to see how he was doing.

DAVE. His suspension, it's, well, I got the decision on it today, there's going to be an investigation, and then well, I don't know. He'll be getting a letter. Not supposed to but we're mates aren't we? Had to come round, let him know as soon as.

ALEX. Suspension?

DAVE. *(Beat.)* He didn't tell you?

ALEX. When did it happen? I don't, ah... what did he do?

DAVE. He never told you about the boy? *(Beat.)* That one got to him, he... things were missed, evidence got lost and/

ALEX. /No, can't be, that's not Tommy, you know that. He's precise, exact, dots every I, crosses every T.

DAVE. Not this time.

ALEX. And this boy...? Seven years Tommy's been doing this, hundreds of cases, hundreds of people... what was different about this one, this boy?

DAVE. Really vicious crime this one, the young man's parents they were killed, stabbed to death. But we can't prove anything against him.

ALEX. So why suspend Tommy?

DAVE. This boy, we know he did it, just can't prove it, not now. The knife's gone, misplaced en-route to the station Tommy said. And this boy he knows just how to play it. Won't be able to hold him on anything. After what he did and we'll have to let him go. *(Beat.)* But it's not just that, it's like, when he's talking to you it's like he's been coached Alex. Like he's got it all up there waiting for the questions he knows are coming. How can he know, be so sure?

ALEX. Tommy wouldn't, I know, he'd never do that.

DAVE. Old Tommy maybe, but lately I don't know. He's been different, distant, drinking too much.

ALEX. A vicious crime you said. Makes sense then he's been knocking back a fair bit. Not sure I blame him, case like that you'd do the same.

DAVE. Not on duty I wouldn't.

ALEX. Neither would Tommy.

DAVE. Other day I asked him about the knife, if it really got nicked out of the back of the car while he was on refs like he said. Tommy just said how this kid was heroic.

ALEX. Heroic?

DAVE. Yeah, and how what he'd done was self defence, understandable. How if this kid got jail time he'd be a hypocrite to be the one to put him there. A hypocrite in uniform he said. He rambled on and on like that. Thing was it was only about eleven a.m. in the morning, only been on duty a few hours and already I could smell the booze on him.

ALEX. I don't believe you.

DAVE. He's coming apart Alex.

ALEX. No, no he/

DAVE. /How can you not see it?

ALEX. *(Beat.)* God you've noticed too.

DAVE. Not just me.

ALEX. What've they been saying?

DAVE. Not much, but enough. I don't want to doubt him but/

ALEX. /Oh God, he couldn't bear that, everything out there to be picked over, laughed at.

DAVE. No one's laughing.

ALEX. I couldn't bear it.

DAVE. Can't believe he didn't tell you, been going through all this alone.

ALEX. I needed time, you know, away from here, away from him, I didn't realise.

DAVE. How could you?

ALEX. Why didn't he tell me, he must've known I wouldn't have done what I did if he'd have just said. Told me what was going on.

DAVE. Maybe that's why.

ALEX. No, he asked me to stay, begged me, didn't want/

DAVE. /Couldn't have you here maybe, couldn't drag you down with him.

ALEX. But surely they know he's not that stupid, they don't think... If he says this knife was stolen then it was stolen.

DAVE. They don't know what to think.

ALEX. And you?

DAVE. A year ago yes, I would've... would've...

ALEX. What?

DAVE. Stuck up for him, one hundred percent.

ALEX. Not now though?

DAVE. Look, you admitted he's not himself, I don't know what's going on with him right now. He doesn't talk.

ALEX. No.

DAVE. Just clams up when I try and/

ALEX. /With me too.

(Pause.)

(Looks at her watch.) Don't know where he's got to but
you'll have to go.

DAVE. Don't hold this against me Alex.

ALEX. Dave, I'm late.

DAVE. You admitted yourself, he's not being straight.

ALEX. Dave.

DAVE. Alex come on, I don't want to fall out over this.

ALEX. I don't think you have a choice.

DAVE. Alex? *(Beat.)* I'll be back again, when he's in next
time. Anyway it's been decided now, they're sending the
letter.

ALEX. If you have anything to say to my husband I think
you should speak to our lawyer.

DAVE. You don't have a lawyer.

ALEX. No, but we'll get one, then you need to speak to
them.

DAVE. This, me being here, like I said it's not official I'm
just... we've been friends for years Alex, there's no need
for any of that.

ALEX. I think it'd be best.

DAVE. Is that what Tommy wants?

ALEX. Tommy wants what I want.

> *(**ALEX** holds the front door open for him.)*

DAVE. I'm sorry about all this.

> *(**ALEX** does not acknowledge his words in any
> way.)*

> *(Exit **DCI LONGMAN**. As the door shuts behind
> him **ALEX** loses her composure and sinks into
> an armchair at a loss as to how to respond*

to these revelations about **TOMMY**. *However,*
before even a minute has elapsed she is on
her feet again looking for the lost item, she
occasionally glances at the wall clock, aware
that she is getting later and later for work. A
set of keys can be heard in the front door and
TOMMY *enters.)*

ALEX. Where were you?

TOMMY. *(Surprised at the forcefulness of her question.)*
What's wrong?

ALEX. Nothing, just, I missed you that's all.

TOMMY. You missed me?

ALEX. Aren't I allowed?

TOMMY. Course *(He kisses her.).*

ALEX. *(Sees the plastic bag in* **TOMMY**'s *hand containing a*
four pack of beer and with a bottle of vodka poking out
of the top.) Don't drink too much tonight okay? You've
been doing that far too much lately. Can I borrow your
house keys? Can't find mine.

TOMMY. How long you back for?

ALEX. Don't know. We'll see how it goes?

TOMMY. Would be so great if you were back for good.

ALEX. Tommy.

TOMMY. Here *(Throws her his house keys.)*

ALEX. *(Picks up her nurse's uniform from the armchair*
and readies to leave.) Oh, almost forgot, you'll have to
make some dinner for you and Hannah, I didn't have
time to do anything.

TOMMY. She was supposed to be staying over at Sarah's
tonight.

ALEX. Sarah's ill, so she can't.

*(***TOMMY*** *remains silent.)*

Last night you said you'd try with Hannah.

TOMMY. No, no, course. Like I said, you come back and I'll be what you want me to be. A proper dad to her.

ALEX. Well I came back.

TOMMY. Think she'd want to go to the park, or see a film or something?

ALEX. Relax, she's a teenager, she'll probably be on the phone all night. Can't believe it, six years of telling you and it took my walking out to make you finally believe it. *(She kisses him.)* Your hands not his, your life not his.

TOMMY. Yeah my life, our life. Nothing to do with him.

> *(Silence. During this* ***ALEX*** *smoothes out the wrinkles in her nurse's uniform, and takes great care in doing so, she concentrates far too hard on this simple task.)*

ALEX. Everything okay at work?

TOMMY. Work um, yeah, ah, it's okay, same as ever.

ALEX. All going alright then?

TOMMY. *(***TOMMY*** *nods his head slightly as he answers.)* Um, er, yeah. Finally been forced to take all those holiday days I had owing.

ALEX. Holiday?

TOMMY. Yeah, said either I take them or lose them so here I am.

> *(Beat.* ***ALEX*** *looks directly at* ***TOMMY***, *neither of them speak.)*

(Glances at the wall clock.) Aren't you gonna be late?

ALEX. Yeah, I ...ahh, I, yeah, see you later.

(As **ALEX** *exits* **TOMMY** *attempts to give her a goodbye kiss, she rejects this and turns away from him.* **ALEX** *exits.* **TOMMY** *sits down on the sofa and takes out a four pack of lager from the plastic shopping bag he was carrying. He opens one and sets the rest at his feet. He begins drinking.)*

(Lights down.)

Scene Sixteen

(Later on that evening. Music can be heard off – it is slightly muffled as it comes from upstairs. TOMMY *sits on the sofa. Two beer cans are at his feet and the bottle of vodka is a third gone and on a side table next to him. A knock is heard at the front door. The sound rouses* TOMMY *a little, he gets slowly to his feet – the effects of the drink are noticeable in his movements.* TOMMY *goes to open the door. He opens it and immediately* KELLY *enters. The two stand in the doorway and watch each other, each unsure how to respond.)*

KELLY. Let me out din't they.

TOMMY. Bail?

KELLY. Yeah.

TOMMY. You shouldn't be here.

KELLY. Yeah.

*(*TOMMY *still does not invite* KELLY *any further into the room.)*

TOMMY. What are you doing? Could revoke your bail for this, put me even further in the shit.

KELLY. Had to talk to you ask you/

TOMMY. /How did you find where I live?

KELLY. Followed Dumbo.

TOMMY. What?

---

* A licence to produce SAFE HOUSE does not include a performance licence for any third-party or copyrighted music. Licensees should create an original composition or use music in the public domain. For further information, please see Music Use Note on page iii.

KELLY. They let me out this dinner time, and I saw that big bloke with the fuck off ears. Doesn't say much. He was walking off one way and I thought why not and went after him.

TOMMY. Why would you do that?

KELLY. Dunno.

TOMMY. So you just followed Dave?

KELLY. Kind of. Didn't know he was coming here though, I swear just went after him wherever you know.

TOMMY. You've gotta leave, my daughter's upstairs.

KELLY. You got a kid?

TOMMY. Kelly, trust me this isn't a good idea.

KELLY. *(Looking over **TOMMY**'s shoulder and moving around him to enter the room, he picks up the bottle of vodka and turns back to **TOMMY**.)* Give us a drink.

TOMMY. What are you doing? Get out now before, before I/

KELLY. /What, you call the police? *(Laughs.)*

TOMMY. Right that's it get the fuck out now *(**TOMMY** bodily forces **KELLY** towards the front door but **KELLY** resists.)*

KELLY. It's happening just like you said. It's happening and I can't make it stop.

                    *(**TOMMY** releases **KELLY**.)*

TOMMY. What can I do?

KELLY. He's in my head, they buried him last week but he's still in there.

TOMMY. I can't get him out.

KELLY. *(He sits. Sounds completely exhausted.)* And you know. I was so sure you could.

TOMMY. I've already done enough for you.

    (Beat.)

You need to talk to someone.

KELLY. I am.

TOMMY. Someone else.

KELLY. After what I did, what I'm gonna get away with, who am I gonna talk to?

    (**TOMMY** *pours a drink for them both – they both drink in silence for a few moments.)*

Why did you help me?

TOMMY. Couldn't not.

KELLY. You're fucked now coz of it. *(Beat.)* Sorry.

TOMMY. Forget him Kelly. Don't hang on to it.

KELLY. It's hanging onto me. I try not to think about him but it won't shift. I picture it, how he was after, fat and dead and bloody and I/

TOMMY. / I can't do this.

KELLY. Thing is, I thought you'd know see, what I'm 'sposed to do now.

    (**TOMMY** *remains silent.)*

You saw inside me, knew how it would be for me after. I thought it'd be different but I'm still that person, hating him yeah, but hating me even more.

TOMMY. *(Getting up from where he is sitting and moving away from* **KELLY**.*)* You can't just come here and say that. What right do you have to come to me and say that?

    (**TOMMY** *pours another large drink and paces and drinks. As he does so he talks to*

*himself. This continual disjointed chatter
varies greatly in volume from a whisper to
shouting.)*

You've got no right. *(Beat.)* Come here and say that to
me. *(Beat.)* To me. No right, to come here, to sneakily
come here and put all of this on me.

(**KELLY** *watches him and as* **TOMMY** *quiets
and stands watching him* **KELLY** *gets up to
leave.*)

KELLY. I should go.

TOMMY. *(Drunkenly.)* I thought you wanted to talk? Talk,
I'm hearing you.

KELLY. You can't hear anyone through your own shit.

TOMMY. Wait.

KELLY. You said yourself, I had no right to come.

TOMMY. I see you. *(Beat.)* Right to your core, even the bits
you can't explain.

KELLY. Well I see you Mr policeman, and you might be
even more fucked up, more damaged than I am.

(*As* **KELLY** *leaves* **TOMMY**'*s house* **TOMMY**
shouts after him.)

TOMMY. That's right you just fuck off, what do I need you
for?

(*As the lights fade* **TOMMY** *sits and opens
another can of lager and drinks.*)

(*Lights down.*)

Scene Seventeen

(Even later that night. Lights up. The light in the room is dim as the room is now only illuminated by one shaded table lamp. Time has passed but **TOMMY** *is still on the sofa in the living room, he is slouched in his seat, cans from the four pack of lager lie empty at his feet. The three-quarters empty bottle of vodka is on the table beside him; he draws a glass full of vodka to his lips. He burps and takes another long swig from the glass.* **HANNAH** *enters the living room and turning on the main living room light she is startled to see him there.)*

TOMMY. Turn that off!

HANNAH. Sorry.

TOMMY. Things look better in the dark.

*(***HANNAH*** turns off the light. Beat.)*

HANNAH. Didn't think you were home. *(As* **HANNAH** *speaks with* **TOMMY** *she goes around the living room looking through the piles of magazines that lie at various places around the room collecting up all of her own* She *magazines from amongst her mother's* Reader's Digest *and* Marie Claire *magazines. She has collected a pile of six or seven by the end of the scene.)*

*(***TOMMY*** slurs his words in the following exchange.)*

TOMMY. What do you want?

HANNAH. Why're you always such an arsehole?

TOMMY. Hey you, language.

HANNAH. Hey you, you're spilling that on the carpet.

TOMMY. Shit. *(He puts the glass down on the floor.)*

HANNAH. Mum'll be pissed. And you're hammered, again.

TOMMY. She'll never know.

HANNAH. Really?

TOMMY. Bitch.

    (Beat.)

HANNAH. What's it worth?

TOMMY. *(Gets up and starts opening all the windows in the room as he speaks.) (Beat. Indicates the bottle.)* Got some of this left.

HANNAH. Fuck off!

TOMMY. *(Takes out his wallet.)* Twenty quid? Here.

HANNAH. *(She watches him warily but does not take the money.)* Gonna cost you more than that.

TOMMY. *(Throws the twenty pound note on the floor at her feet in disgust.)* Scheming bitch.

HANNAH. Sorry what was that Daddy dearest, didn't quite get that.

TOMMY. Yeah you did.

    (Beat.)

Don't call me that.

HANNAH. What Daddy or dearest?

TOMMY. You know.

HANNAH. Don't worry Tommy, far as I'm concerned you're not even good stepdad material. Case you were wondering I don't lie awake at night wishing and wanting oh ever so much to be your kid. I know what happens to your kids.

TOMMY. *(**TOMMY** confronts her pulling himself up to his full height.)* You don't talk about that.

HANNAH. Why not coz you say so? Poor fuckin' kid, two years old and it's like she never existed. You've cleaned out nearly all of her room, all her stuff, almost erased her. *(Beat.)* And all you had to do was check on her.

TOMMY. You don't know what you're talking about.

HANNAH. Hey look, just saying that's all. It was just you and Rosie in the house, she chokes to death and you're just sitting here, getting fucking plastered as usual. You ignored her when all you had to do/

> *(**TOMMY**'s surprised **HANNAH** believes this of him. It slightly sobers him up.)*

TOMMY. / is that what you think? I didn't ignore her.

HANNAH. What would you call it?

TOMMY. Your mum knew, she left me in the house alone with Rosie and all the time she knew.

HANNAH. Knew what?

TOMMY. When it was just... just me and Rosie I didn't go in, your mother she knew I'd wait for her.

HANNAH. Why?

TOMMY. Just would.

HANNAH. Rosie was your daughter too, it wasn't only up to Mum to/

TOMMY. /Didn't like being alone in there with her that's all.

HANNAH. What were you so scared of?

> *(**TOMMY** remains silent.)*

Must be/

TOMMY. /She was my girl and I/

HANNAH. /I'm your girl, well kind of. So what, you scared of me?

>*(Beat.)*

TOMMY. *(He backs* **HANNAH** *into a corner as he speaks.)* What do you want from me? Why you being such a bitch?

HANNAH. *(Backing away from him until she is trapped in a corner.)* I ... uh... didn't uh... mean... I didn't mean anything. I ...

TOMMY. What do you really want?

HANNAH. Leave me alone. (**HANNAH** *drops the pile of magazines she has collected to the floor.)*

>*(***TOMMY** *no response, he just stares at her.)*

What? Don't... stop, stop looking at me like that... Tommy I ...

>*(***TOMMY** *he continues to stare.)*

Look I'm sorry, Tommy what are you... stop it.

TOMMY. You're beautiful. Your Auntie Steph was the same when she was your age.

HANNAH. Tommy?

TOMMY. Tried to keep her safe, trying to keep you/

HANNAH. Did you hate her too then; Auntie Steph?

TOMMY. Don't hate you.

HANNAH. Never get close like this. Not to me, ever.

>*(***TOMMY** *steps back from the closeness to* **HANNAH.***)*

Dad's aren't supposed to hate their kids.

TOMMY. You don't understand Han/

HANNAH. Can never bear to be close to me. (*HANNAH's crying now.*)

TOMMY. You're precious Hannah. You and Rosie.

HANNAH. Just saying that.

TOMMY. No.

HANNAH. Don't want your money. Won't tell Mum. Was never going to really.

TOMMY. Don't know how to fix things.

HANNAH. Should know; you're the Dad. My Dad. Sort of.

(*Beat.*)

TOMMY. I just don't... (*Hesitant.*) Can I, if you don't mind, um, can I hug you?

HANNAH. (*Shocked.*) Yeah?

TOMMY. If you don't mind.

(*HANNAH lets him. TOMMY hugs HANNAH tentatively. She squeezes him tight. He hugs her properly then.*)

(*After a few moments TOMMY breaks free of HANNAH.*)

HANNAH. I like you like this.

TOMMY. You're right, I've got to fix things. Properly.

(*TOMMY grabs his keys, puts his shoes on and prepares to leave.*)

HANNAH. Where you going? It's the middle of the night and you're still practically off your face.

(*TOMMY stops a moment and gives his full attention to HANNAH.*)

TOMMY. It's the only thing I know how to do that'll keep everyone safe.

HANNAH. But Tommy, what does that/

TOMMY. Trust me.

       (**TOMMY** *rushes out of the house.*)

       (*Lights down.*)

Scene Eighteen

(Two days later. Lights up. Early morning – ~~*8.30*~~*a.m.* **DAVE** *sits across the table from* **TOMMY.** *They are in a police interrogation room, the ~~same~~ one as the previous scenes between* **TOMMY** *and* **KELLY.** ~~**DAVE**~~ *is dressed in his* **DCI** *police uniform, as in Scene Fourteen, while* **TOMMY** *is wearing civilian clothes. There is a police interrogation recording device present.* **TOMMY** *has just finished giving a lengthy statement.)*

*(***DAVE*** turns off the tape recorder before he speaks. It remains off throughout the following.)*

(Pause. The two men watch each other.)

DAVE. I arranged for this, thought it'd be easier here, you know?

TOMMY. Easier?

DAVE. Steph wants to see you.

TOMMY. No.

DAVE. But she's/

TOMMY. /I said no.

*(Beat. ***TOMMY*** paces.)*

What about Alex, has she...

DAVE. In time she'll *(Thinks better of what he is saying and changes tack.),* Give her time yeah.

*(***TOMMY*** gets up and paces in the small room.)*

TOMMY. No *(Beat.)* she won't, Hannah won't either. And I don't blame them, how can I?

DAVE. Steph's here, outside, waiting.

>   *(Pause – neither speaks. **TOMMY** returns to his seat.)*

Will you see her?

>   *(**STEPH** rushes in from where she has been waiting outside the room before **TOMMY** can answer.)*

STEPH. Sorry Dave, I couldn't wait outside. I knew he'd say no if you asked him *(Beat.)* Tommy I had to see you.

TOMMY. Ah sis. *(He does not continue but instead puts his face in his hands.)*

DAVE. I'll just, um. Steph are you alright to um…

STEPH. For God sake it's Tommy I'll be okay Dave.

DAVE. But, um, I'll be outside. We ah, ten minutes okay? If anyone finds out I let you in here like this Steph. I don't even want to think about that.

>   *(**DAVE** exits. **STEPH** approaches the chair opposite **TOMMY** cautiously and sits down. **TOMMY** remains with his head in his hands and does not acknowledge her. **STEPH** slowly and gently removes **TOMMY**'s hands from his face. He looks at her, his expression is neutral.)*

STEPH. Are they um…

TOMMY. Why did you come sis?

STEPH. Did they give you something to eat? I know sometimes these places *(She trails off as she speaks and gets quieter and quieter.)* they don't give you enough.

TOMMY. Why'd you come? I said not to.

STEPH. Ha, I got a real job if you can believe that. In a florists, me a florist. It's only three days a week but/

TOMMY. /I told you not to come.

(*Beat.*)

STEPH. Had to.

TOMMY. How's Hannah? I hope she's not (*Beat.*) Tell her it may not look like it, but this'll fix things. (*Beat.*) Why you here?

STEPH. Love you don't I? Always. Important that having someone love you.

(*Pause.*)

Where were you? All yesterday didn't know where you'd gone, no one did.

TOMMY. Needed to walk, think about things.

STEPH. When Dave called, said you'd ended up here, didn't know what to think.

(*Beat.*)

TOMMY. He's inside me Steph. Made me so scared I'd do those things too/ made me

STEPH. /You could never. I know that, always known that.

TOMMY. I was never sure. So you see I have to. (*Beat.*) When I stabbed him, it was really me I was hurting. Consigning myself to the memory of that, the knowledge that I could do that, kill him like that. From then until now I haven't been able to be, to have anything normal, be normal. We've, both of us, lost so much since then. Rosie and and, and...

STEPH. Yeah.

(*Beat.*)

TOMMY. But dad, he didn't die though, not back then. I couldn't kill him I wasn't strong enough.

STEPH. I saw you stab him, helped you after, both of us together. Buried him deep Tommy.

TOMMY. He's inside me, part of both of us, maybe if we can just, just…

STEPH. We're not meant to be happy Tommy, can't be after what we did.

TOMMY. If we say what we did and/

STEPH. /What?

>   *(Beat.)*

TOMMY. *(He speaks quietly, as if not wanting her to hear his words.)* Say what we did to him.

>   *(Pause.* **TOMMY** *will not look at* **STEPH.***)*

STEPH. Tommy?

>   *(Beat.)*

Oh God what did you do?

>   *(***TOMMY** *remains silent.)*

Did you say?

>   *(Beat.)*

You had no right. Wasn't just your secret.

TOMMY. Had to, to say the words. This is what I did, why I did. Not just thinking about it, about him, over and over for years but finally saying the words.

STEPH. And what about me Tommy?

TOMMY. Ten years and this thing I did, I can't forget it.

STEPH. What do I do now Tommy?

TOMMY. Do you want to always keep that inside? Let the memory of what he did and how we made him stop eat you up, until what? You try again? I won't be there anymore Steph to find you in time.

STEPH. Tommy.

TOMMY. Can't be happy Steph, not like this. But wanted to try, for once say everything and try.

STEPH. I'm a florist now Tommy.

TOMMY. Be happy Steph. Be grounded, ordinary.

STEPH. I'm gonna learn flower arranging.

TOMMY. I stabbed him, killed him. That's what I did, what we did.

STEPH. A fucking florist, can you believe it?

TOMMY. *(He reaches across the table and takes both of her hands in his.)* Together. You were there Steph, helping me.

> *(Beat.* **STEPH** *looks at* **TOMMY**, *she is terrified by him.)*

STEPH. Three days a week I'm a florist Tommy.

TOMMY. For once say everything, to someone other than me, say what happened.

STEPH. They've said, six months and I'll be arranging the flowers Tommy.

> *(Beat – they both watch each other.)*

> *(Lights down. Blackout.)*

The End

ABOUT THE AUTHOR

Lorna French is a playwright, writing workshop leader and dramaturg. Lorna has most recently presented a reading of *Esther* at Jermyn Street Theatre in March 2022. *Jacaranda* was produced by Pentabus Theatre and Theatre by the Lake for a tour of rural venues in 2021. She also wrote for Limbik Theatre and the HearMe Now monologue series (via Titilola Dawudu and Tamasha Theatre Company) in 2021. She wrote the short play *I See You Now*, produced as part of the 15 Heroines plays at Jermyn Street Theatre in November 2020. Also the short radio drama *NFA* for Menagerie Theatre Company and the University of Cambridge in October 2020. *Esther*, a play about Black African Caribbean women of Birmingham and the West Midlands, was inspired by oral history interviews with several local women. It was shortlisted for the Theatre Uncut Political Playwriting Award 2020 and longlisted for the Women's Prize for Playwriting 2020. Esther received a staged reading at Midlands Arts Centre (MAC) in 2019 made possible by a Developing Your Creative Practice award from Arts Council England.

Other past work includes *The Last Flag*, a co-written Afternoon Drama for BBC Radio 4 and Eclipse Theatre Company in 2018 and a co-written adaptation of *Jane Eyre* for Bolton Octagon, also in 2018. In 2017, Lorna wrote a one-act play called *Transitions* for Birmingham Rep Education Department and RSA Academy. In 2016, she wrote an audio drama called *You Say* for the White Open Spaces monologues co-commissioned by Eclipse and Pentabus Theatre. Lorna is a two-time winner of the Alfred Fagon Award (in 2006 and 2016) and has presented work at, or written work for, Birmingham Rep, Oval House, MAC, Young Vic and New Wolsey Theatre.

Lorna is currently mentoring a writer for Red Talent Management and also working with the National Theatre's Education Department on New Views. This involves working with young people writing plays in secondary schools in the Midlands and London. She is also working as a Lead Writer for Writing West Midlands running monthly Sparks writing workshops with young people. She has previously worked as an Associate Lecturer on the Writing for Performance MA and other BA Performing Arts Undergraduate programmes at the University of Derby. She has also worked as a dramaturg on *Close to the Edge* by Viv Manjaro (Planet Arts and Red Earth Collective) and on *Revealed* by Daniel Anderson (Rites of Passage Productions).

Lightning Source UK Ltd.
Milton Keynes UK
UKHW020409070622
404044UK00003B/7